MacArthur Competence Assessment Tool for Clinical Research (MacCAT-CR)

Paul S. Appelbaum and Thomas Grisso

Law and Psychiatry Program
University of Massachusetts Medical School
Worcester, MA

Developed under the auspices of the
John D. and Catherine T. MacArthur Foundation
Research Network on Mental Health and the Law

D1234173

Professional Resource Press
Sarasota, FL

Published by Professional Resource Press
(An imprint of Professional Resource Exchange, Inc.)
Post Office Box 3197
Sarasota, FL 34230-3197

Printed in the United States of America

This publication is sold with the understanding that the Publisher is not engaged in rendering professional services. If legal, psychological, medical, accounting, or other expert advice or assistance is sought or required, the reader should seek the services of a competent professional.

The copy editor for this book was Judith Warinner, the managing editor was Debbie Fink, and the cover and text designer was Laurie Girsch.

Library of Congress Cataloging-in-Publication Data

Appelbaum, Paul S.
    MacArthur competence assessment tool for clinical research (MacCAT-CR) / Paul S. Appelbaum and Thomas Grisso.
        p. ; cm.
    Includes bibliographical references.
    ISBN-13: 978-1-56887-071-7 / ISBN-10: 1-56887-071-X (alk. paper)
        1. Human experimentation in medicine. 2. Informed consent (Medical law) 3. Patient participation. I. Title: MacCAT-CR. II. Grisso, Thomas. III. Title.
    [DNLM: 1. Patient Selection. 2. Research. 3. Decision Making. 4. Informed Consent. 5. Mental Competency. 6. Patient Participation--psychology. WM 20 A646m 2001]
    R853.H8 A675 2001

                                                            2001031638

PREFACE

The *MacArthur Competence Assessment Tool for Clinical Research (MacCAT-CR)* is a structured interview schedule for assessing decision-making abilities relevant for judgments about subjects' competence to consent to participation in research. It is derived from a companion instrument, the *MacArthur Competence Assessment Tool for Treatment (MacCAT-T)*, also published by Professional Resource Press (Grisso & Appelbaum, 1998b). Both MacCATs owe their existence to the MacArthur Treatment Competence Project, a program of research on informed consent and patients' decision-making capacities funded by the John D. and Catherine T. MacArthur Foundation through its Research Network on Mental Health and the Law. We are grateful to the other members of the Network for their support and assistance with this work.

Development of the MacCAT-CR was stimulated by enormous public and professional interest during the last decade in the ethics of research with human subjects. Among the areas of concern has been the competence of potential research subjects to make decisions regarding their participation in projects that may pose some degree of risk to them. This is particularly the case when subjects suffer from conditions that can impair their decision-making capacities without rendering them obviously incompetent to make decisions. Such conditions may include some of the more severe mental illnesses, the early stages of dementing disorders such as Alzheimer's disease, and serious medical disorders that either impair mentation directly or that call for the use of treatments that may affect mental functioning. Concern about the decisional capacity of potential research subjects was exemplified by the report on the topic from the National Bioethics Advisory Commission (NBAC), which called for mandatory competence assessment by an independent evaluator for all subjects suffering from mental disorders that may impair cognition (NBAC, 1998).

Although NBAC's recommendations have yet to acquire the force of law, in the wake of the Commission's report, Institutional Review Boards (IRBs)—which were charged with protecting human subjects—began to inquire more closely into how investigators intended to insure that incompetent subjects would not be permitted to enter their research projects. Many researchers themselves sought means of assessing the decisional capacities of potential subjects. Yet, almost no instruments for this purpose existed, and those that did had not demonstrated either utility or validity.

In the midst of broadening concern about these matters, we realized that the model for capacity assessment that we had developed in the MacCAT-T might be modifiable for the purpose of assessing capacities in the research setting. Thus, the MacCAT-CR was born. Initially used as a research tool to explore the competence of various subject groups (Appelbaum et al., 1999; Carpenter et al., 2000; Kim et al., 2001), it proved to be adaptable to a variety of research projects, easy to administer (requiring 15-20 minutes for most subjects), and reliable to score. As research with the MacCAT-CR continued, the instrument began to be adopted by investigators seeking assurance regarding the decisional capacities of their subjects. It was this growing use of the MacCAT-CR that led us to the publication of this manual.

Readers should be cautioned, however, that the MacCAT-CR manual itself does not provide all of the information that they will need to perform valid competence assessments. Users of the MacCAT-CR must also know something of the meaning of informed consent, the role of competence in determining whose decisions will be respected, and the legal and clinical framework in which judgments about subjects' competence must be made. Much of this background is described in our book, *Assessing Competence to Consent to Treatment: A Guide for Physicians and Other Health Professionals* (Grisso & Appelbaum, 1998a). Additional background information regarding informed consent to research can be found in *Informed Consent: Legal Theory and Clinical Practice* (Berg et al., 2001) and in the chapter by Berg and Appelbaum (1999) that is reprinted in Appendix C of this manual (pp. 45-84).

We are pleased to be able to make the MacCAT-CR widely available to the clinical research community. It is our hope that by enabling the identification of subjects with impaired capacities, the MacCAT-CR will encourage investigators to modify their consent procedures to allow even these subjects to make competent decisions for themselves (Carpenter et al., 2000), rather than being deprived of their decision-making rights. Along with the exclusion from participation of potential subjects who are unable to render a competent consent even under optimal circumstances, these practices—facilitated by the MacCAT-CR—should allow both greater protection of human subjects and the conduct of legitimate clinical research untainted by concerns regarding recruitment of incompetent subjects.

Paul S. Appelbaum
Thomas Grisso
Worcester, Massachusetts
August, 2001

TABLE OF CONTENTS

II. INTERVIEW *(Continued)*

III. RATING   17

APPENDIX C: Subjects' Capacity to Consent to
            Neurobiological Research *(Continued)*

MacArthur Competence Assessment Tool for Clinical Research (MacCAT-CR)

INTRODUCTION

The *MacArthur Competence Assessment Tool for Clinical Research (MacCAT-CR)* provides a semistructured interview format with which clinical researchers can assess and rate the abilities of potential research subjects in four areas that represent part of the standard for competence to consent to research in most jurisdictions:

1. *understanding* of disclosed information about the nature of the research project and its procedures
2. *appreciation* of the effects of research participation (or failure to participate) on subjects' own situations
3. *reasoning* in the process of deciding about participation, focusing on subjects' abilities to compare alternatives in light of their consequences
4. *expressing a choice* about research participation

These four areas of ability that are assessed by the MacCAT-CR were identified by comprehensive reviews of the legal and ethical standards for competence to consent to treatment and research (Appelbaum & Grisso, 1988, 1995; Appelbaum & Roth, 1982; Berg, Appelbaum, & Grisso, 1996). Complete definitions of these ability concepts and case examples to illustrate them are provided in *Assessing Competence to Consent to Treatment: A Guide for Physicians and Other Health Professionals* (Grisso & Appelbaum, 1998a).

An assessment of these abilities is essential (depending on the legal criteria for decision-making competence in effect in a particular jurisdiction), but may not be sufficient for making judgments about a subject's competence to decide about participation in research. To reach valid conclusions about a subject's competence, MacCAT-CR information may need to be supplemented with information about the subject's diagnoses and mental status, as well as knowledge of the medical and social circumstances in which the subject's decision is being made. The possibility that subjects' performances can be improved by modifying informational procedures should always be considered.

The MacCAT-CR provides a format for disclosure of *selected* information that describes the research project. A standard set of questions is asked to sample subjects' abilities to understand and appreciate the information, to reason about it, and to express a choice. Neither disclosures nor questions are meant to be exhaustive with regard to relevant information that is required to be disclosed, or that might be desirable for subjects to understand or appreciate, in full informed consent procedures. The MacCAT-CR samples subjects' abilities with regard to representative content, rather than testing them on the full content of a typical informed consent disclosure.

The MacCAT-CR is based on the structure of the *MacArthur Competence Assessment Tool for Treatment (MacCAT-T*; Grisso & Appelbaum, 1998b), with changes to make it better suited to the research setting. Although there is some overlap, the two instruments will not necessarily yield identical results in the same subjects. (When subjects' basic competence to consent to treatment is in question, investigators recruiting subjects into research involving treatment methods may elect to screen potential subjects with the MacCAT-T.) The number of questions in each section and their foci have been modified from the MacCAT-T to better fit the context of a research setting. Scoring ranges may vary from those in the MacCAT-T.

Unlike the MacCAT-T, the MacCAT-CR does not have to be individualized for each subject, although it will need to be individualized for each research project. (This is true as long as projects have consistent procedures for every subject.) Thus, both research and routine use of the MacCAT-CR should be easier than use of the MacCAT-T. The framework of the MacCAT-CR should prove adaptable to all clinical trials and most other interventional research with patient populations. Modified versions, eliminating sections that are not relevant in particular contexts, may be applicable to other forms of research as well.

The MacCAT-CR rating criteria provide a way for the clinician to express opinions concerning the adequacy or inadequacy of each of the subject's responses. A summary of the subject's ratings for questions within a particular type of ability provides an indication of the adequacy or degree of deficits in the subject's abilities to deal with information and decisions about research participation. However, the MacCAT-CR does not provide "cut-off scores" that represent "competence" or "incompetence" on the four abilities. This is because the MacCAT-CR was designed to be consistent with a basic maxim in the legal definition of competence: No particular level of ability is always determinative of competence or incompetence across all subjects, all disorders, and all medical or research situations. (See Chapter 2 in Grisso and Appelbaum, 1998a, for an explanation of this maxim as well as others that are important for understanding legal competencies.)

Moreover, the MacCAT-CR does not provide an overall "MacCAT-CR total score." It provides ratings on each of the four areas of decisional ability described earlier, but does not sum these scores. This is related to another basic concept of competence: In some cases, a serious deficit in ability in any one of the four areas may translate to a clinical opinion of incompetence, even if the subject's capacities in the other three areas are quite adequate.

The MacCAT-CR interview process involves two steps: the *Interview* itself, and *Rating* of the subject's performance on interview inquiry questions. These are described in the following sections, after a description of how the MacCAT-CR can be customized to the circumstances of particular research projects.

I.
CUSTOMIZING THE
MacCAT-CR

The MacCAT-CR provides a format for the assessment of capacities related to consent to research participation. For optimal use, the MacCAT-CR should be customized to reflect the details of the particular research project to which subjects are being asked to consent. (In some circumstances, for example, when subjects' decisional competence is itself the focus of research, the version of the MacCAT-CR that is used may be based on a hypothetical study.) The customization process involves identifying information from the research project at hand that conforms to the categories of information specified in the MacCAT-CR format.

Understanding Section

The five subparts of the Understanding section are described in Section II: Interview (pp. 9-10). Information relevant to each of the subparts should be identified and utilized for each disclosure. Insofar as possible, the format of the examples in the Sample MacCAT-CR Interview (pp. 29-39) should be followed. It is important to remember that these disclosures are intended to provide *samples* of the kind of information contained in an informed consent disclosure. Including all of the extensive information typically disclosed to subjects in each of these categories will confound the assessment process. Generally, it is not desirable to excerpt content directly from consent forms, since the material on these forms tends to be more extensive in scope and more complex in language than is desirable here. We recommend that MacCAT-CR disclosures be geared to an 8th-grade reading level, unless the characteristics of the population involved suggest otherwise. (Most word processing programs now contain functions allowing reading level to be assessed easily.)

In general, investigators and others drafting a customized MacCAT-CR will want to use the same number of Understanding questions in each subpart as specified here. This will allow comparison of results with published data and with other projects using the MacCAT-CR. There may be occasions, however, when the nature of a specific research project (e.g., when unusually simple methods are being used) requires a reduction in the number of questions. This should be noted explicitly if MacCAT-CR scores are reported in presentations or publications.

Appreciation Section

The three Appreciation questions (see Section II, pp. 10-11) are intended to assess the extent to which subjects recognize the impact of research participation on their own care. Subpart 1 will be relevant to almost all research projects. Subparts 2 and 3 are generally relevant, but may require modification or omission in cases when standard research methods are not employed or subjects' ability to receive care outside the study is limited.

Reasoning Section

Modification of the format of this section as described in Section II (pp. 11-12) will not usually be necessary, although the specific information regarding risks and benefits that is included in Subpart 3 must be supplied. When it is difficult to identify everyday consequences of research participation (e.g., in a one-time only questionnaire study) Subpart 3 can be omitted.

Expressing a Choice Section

This section is standardized for all versions of the MacCAT-CR.

II.
INTERVIEW

Content

The MacCAT-CR interview combines disclosure of informed consent information with assessment of subjects' abilities to understand and appreciate the information, and to make decisions about research participation. The structure of the MacCAT-CR is described below. Investigators who are seeking to use the MacCAT-CR to screen potential subjects for entry into their research project will ordinarily want to use this framework to produce a MacCAT-CR version customized for their research project. Researchers investigating the characteristics of decisional capacity *per se* may elect to use a version of the MacCAT-CR that describes a hypothetical research project.

Because the specific information disclosed in a MacCAT-CR procedure will depend on the nature of the research project, the content is described in general terms here. A sample MacCAT-CR disclosure, based on a hypothetical research project, is appended to this manual (see Sample MacCAT-CR Interview, pp. 29-39) and should be read along with the description that follows.

Understanding Section. This section is divided into five subparts.

- *Subpart 1* (4 items) assesses understanding of disclosed information about the nature of the research project. This includes the objective of the project and three of its most important procedural elements, that is, those procedures experienced by subjects who participate in the study (e.g., duration, daily doses of medication, every-other-day interviews, and weekly blood drawing).

- *Subpart 2* (1 item) assesses subjects' abilities to understand that the *primary* purpose of the project is research (i.e., gaining generalized knowledge about a particular topic), rather than the treatment of the research subjects *per se.*

- *Subpart 3* (3 items) assesses subjects' understanding of the effect of research methods on individualized care, that is, *how* the research project differs from ordinary treatment. Three of the most significant elements of the project's methods should be selected for disclosure here.

- *Subpart 4* (4 items) assesses understanding of disclosed information about the potential benefits and risks/discomforts associated with subjects' participation in the project. Disclosure of benefits includes one statement regarding the potential benefits of the generalized knowledge that the research study will produce, and one statement regarding the potential benefits to subjects themselves. If there are no likely benefits to subjects, this should be stated here. Two of the most important potential risks/discomforts (taking into account both magnitude and likelihood) should be disclosed and assessed here as well.

- *Subpart 5* (1 item) addresses subjects' understanding that potential participants can refuse to participate in the study or can withdraw at any time and still receive or be referred for ordinary care (assuming this is true for a given study).

Appreciation Section. This section focuses on subjects' abilities to acknowledge how they themselves will be affected by a decision to participate in the research project. Appreciation questions are predicated on the usual consequences of research using patient populations, including research that is not itself intended to have therapeutic benefit. Questions may need to be modified to the extent that a research project carries greater therapeutic intent (e.g., an open-label trial of a new medication for a condition with no known effective treatment) or allows full individualization of treatment during the course of the study. In addition, the relevance of these questions to research that draws subjects from nonpatient populations will have to be assessed on a case-by-case basis. The appreciation section is divided into three subparts.

- *Subpart 1* assesses subjects' appreciation that the purpose of inviting them to participate in the study is not to optimize their care or well-being. Rather, the goal is to generate new knowledge.
- *Subpart 2* looks at appreciation that methods actually involved in the study may take precedence over individualized care (e.g., use of placebos, randomized assignment, medication protocols, double-blind procedures, etc.). A particular method used in the study is selected for focus here. (In the event that a study employs no methods that constrain individualized decisions about subjects' care, this question may be omitted.)
- *Subpart 3* explores subjects' appreciation that they have an actual ability to decline to participate or to withdraw at a later time, and still receive ordinary clinical care and not otherwise be penalized. (This question will have to be modified when, in fact, this is not the case.)

Reasoning Section. This section is very similar to the corresponding section in the MacCAT-T. It addresses subjects' abilities to compare alternatives in light of their consequences, including the ability to draw inferences about the impact of the study on subjects' daily

11

lives. The choice on which it focuses is whether or not to participate in the research project. (Question R-3, the generating consequences task, is optional. It is likely to be relevant to outpatient, longitudinal research, but may not be relevant to inpatient or some cross-sectional research.) This section is composed of four subparts.

- *Subpart 1* assesses subjects' consequential reasoning, that is, the extent to which they include the potential consequences of their choices in their reasoning processes.
- *Subpart 2* focuses on subjects' comparative reasoning, defined as their abilities to compare the advantages and disadvantages of more than one alternative.
- *Subpart 3* examines subjects' abilities to generate consequences to their everyday lives of participating or not participating in the research project. To enable subjects to respond appropriately, the previously disclosed benefits and risks/discomforts are described again here. This subpart may not be relevant for some research settings and is therefore optional.
- *Subpart 4* is a measure of the logical consistency of the subjects' choices, taking into account the objectives they desire to pursue.

Expressing a Choice Section. This section, which invites subjects to indicate their choice regarding participation in the research project, is adapted directly from the MacCAT-T.

General Procedures

Timing. The MacCAT-CR can be used as a screening instrument prior to the initiation of an informed consent process with potential subjects; or it can be employed after information has been provided to subjects and decisions have been made regarding participation, as a check on the validity of subjects' consent.

Sequence. The interview should proceed in the sequence described previously. Some flexibility is allowable, however, to meet needs of specific subjects, as long as all parts are completed by the end of the interview.

Style. It is important for clinicians to adapt their disclosure and questioning (vocabulary, sentence length, pace) to the verbal abilities, level of intelligence, and emotional needs of the subject.

Recording. Subjects' responses to inquiries should be recorded in the spaces indicated on the interview form (see Sample MacCAT-CR Interview, pp. 29-39). Ratings of the subjects' understanding, appreciation, reasoning, and choice will be made later on the basis of the interviewer's notes in these spaces (see MacCAT-CR Record Form, pp. 41-44).

Duration. For most subjects, the MacCAT-CR takes 15 to 20 minutes to administer. Very impaired subjects who require frequent repetitions of disclosures and multiple probes (see below), however, may require longer periods of time.

Introduction

Describe to the subject the purpose of the interview, framing it as a discussion about the subject's understanding of the research project that he or she has been invited to join. Encourage the subject to ask questions as the interview proceeds.

Understanding Section

Disclosure. Subject should be given a card containing the disclosure for each section and asked to read along as the disclosure is read to him or her. Ask if there are any questions; if there are, answer them.

Inquiry. Take the card from the subject. Tell the subject that you want to make sure he or she has understood what you have described. Ask the subject to describe to you his or her understanding of the information—the purpose of the research project, the procedures involved, and so on. Note responses in the appropriate space on the interview form.

Probe. When subjects' responses omit information for any of the important elements, use a prompt to make inquiry about what they recall and understand concerning that portion of the disclosure. Prompts should be sufficiently general so as not to cue the subject to the information necessary to answer the question. Interviewers should be familiar with the scoring criteria, so probes can be framed appropriately. For example, if the subject does not describe the benefits of the study, prompt: "Tell me what good things might come from your participating in this research project." Note responses on the interview form.

Redisclosure and Reinquiry. If subject has described any of the major elements incorrectly or has omitted any of them even after probing, reread the *entire* disclosure for that section *once* and again inquire concerning the subject's comprehension of the information. Note responses on the interview form. Do not repeat a disclosure more than once.

Appreciation Section

The purpose of this section is to determine whether subjects can acknowledge how they themselves will be affected by a decision to participate in the research project. No disclosure precedes the inquiry in this section.

Inquiry. The basic inquiry is contained on the interview form.

Probe. If subjects offer responses that appear to reflect failure to appreciate the nature of research participation as it relates to their personal situations (see "Appreciation" in "III. Rating," pp. 19-22), follow-up questions should be used to assess the basis for their conclusions. Questions should be framed with the scoring criteria in mind. This will be relevant to later rating of their responses.

Reasoning and Expressing a Choice Sections

As described in the Sample MacCAT-CR Interview (see pp. 29-39), these sections involve a discussion between the interviewer and the subject that explores the subject's choice with regard to research participation and how the subject is arriving at that choice.

Procedure to Establish Subject's Choice. To determine the stability of a subject's choice, he or she is queried twice about his or her preferences, once at the beginning of this section and once again at the end.

Logical Consistency. Interviewers will be asked at the end of the procedure to rate the degree to which the subject's choice is logically consistent with his or her previous reasoning and discussion of the consequences of alternative options. At this point, if the choice is consistent, no further probing is required. If questions exist about the consistency of the choice, the inconsistencies should be discussed with the subject until the interviewer understands the basis for the real or apparent disparity.

III.
RATING

Responses recorded on the interview form provide the content for rating subjects' responses. Guidelines for the rating process are provided below for each of the parts of the MacCAT-CR (Understanding, Appreciation, Reasoning, and Expressing a Choice). Record ratings on the MacCAT-CR Record Form (see pp. 41-44).

Understanding

The following guidelines are used to rate each item in the five Understanding subparts of the MacCAT-CR.

Rating   Guidelines

2   Subject recalls the content of the item and offers a fairly clear version of it. A verbatim repetition of the interviewer's description is not required; in fact, paraphrase in the subject's own words is preferred.

            For *Benefit/Risk* items, the subject must provide a reasonably accurate indication of the likelihood that the ben-

Rating   Guidelines

efit/risk will be experienced, if this was described in the disclosure.

1   Subject shows some recollection of the item content, but describes it in a way that renders understanding uncertain, *even after the interviewer has made efforts to obtain clarification from the subject.*

Examples include responses that could possibly indicate understanding but are too broad or vague for one to be sure (e.g., for purpose of research, "They want to see what will happen."), or responses that contain some specific and correct piece of information but lack some other part of the critical content (e.g., for specific risk, possibility is noted with no indication of likelihood [assuming that has been disclosed]).

0   Subject (a) does not recall the content of the item; or (b) describes it in a way that is clearly inaccurate; or (c) describes it in a way that seriously distorts its meaning, *even after the interviewer has made efforts to obtain clarification from the patient*; or offers a response that is unrelated to the question or unintelligible.

Understanding Summary Ratings

For each of the five Understanding subparts:

- Add the ratings for all items in the subpart. Add them to produce an overall *Understanding Summary Rating*, and enter on the Record Form.

- When a standard version of the MacCAT-CR is used, this produces an Understanding Rating between 0 and 26.

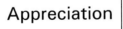
Appreciation

Somewhat different rating guidelines are needed for each of the three subparts in the Appreciation section.

> ### Subpart 1
> ### Goal of recruitment is not to
> ### optimize subject's care or well-being

Rating   Guidelines

2   Subject acknowledges that he or she is being recruited for a valid reason unrelated to potential personal benefit from being in the study (e.g., because he or she has a condition of relevance to the study; because he or she has previously indicated a willingness to help with studies of this sort, etc.).

1   Subject acknowledges being recruited for reasons both related to and unrelated to potential personal benefit.

OR

Subject maintains he or she is being recruited for a reason related only to potential personal benefit, but has a plausible explanation for why this is the case.

<u>Rating</u>   <u>Guidelines</u>

0   Subject maintains he or she is being recruited for a reason related only to potential personal benefit, but does not have a plausible explanation for why this is the case.

OR

Subject offers response that is unrelated to the question or unintelligible.

Subpart 2
Research methods take precedence
over individualized care

<u>Rating</u>   <u>Guidelines</u>

2   Subject provides response consistent with the idea that the research protocol, not personal needs, will determine the experimental condition to which he or she will be assigned. (Example selected to test this will vary according to the procedures of the study in question.)

1   Subject is uncertain whether the research protocol or personal needs will determine the experimental condition to which he or she will be assigned.

OR

Subject believes that personal needs will determine assignment to experimental conditions, but has a plausible explanation for why this might be the case.

Rating	Guidelines

0   Subject believes personal needs will determine assignment to experimental conditions, but does not have a plausible explanation for why this would be the case.

OR

Subject offers a response that is unrelated to the question or unintelligible.

> ***Subpart 3***
> ***Ability to decline or withdraw***
> ***participation***

Rating	Guidelines

2   Subject acknowledges that failure to participate or later withdrawal will not adversely affect him or her (in particular, in the context of a treatment setting, that subject can continue to receive ordinary care, assuming that this is the case).

1   Subject is uncertain whether failure to participate or later withdrawal will adversely affect him or her.

OR

Subject believes failure to participate or later withdrawal will adversely affect him or her and has a plausible explanation for why this is the case.

Rating	Guidelines
0	Subject believes failure to participate or later withdrawal will adversely affect him or her and does not have a plausible explanation for why this is the case.

OR

Subject offers response that is unrelated to the question or unintelligible.

Appreciation Summary Ratings

Add the ratings from the three Appreciation subparts to obtain an Appreciation Summary Rating, which will be between 0 and 6.

─────────────── | **Reasoning** | ───────────────

Again, each of the Reasoning subparts has somewhat different guidelines for rating.

Subpart 1
Consequential Reasoning

Rating	Guidelines
2	Subject mentions at least two specific consequences when explaining the choice.

The consequences may be related to only one or more than one alternative, including alternatives not mentioned in the disclosure.

Rating   Guidelines

1   Subject mentions only one specific consequence when explaining the choice.

0   Subject mentions no specific consequences when explaining the choice, even after being asked directly whether there were "any more specific reasons why that choice seems best."

Subpart 2
Comparative Reasoning

Rating   Guidelines

2   Subject offers at least one statement in the form of a comparison of at least two options, with the comparison including a statement of at least one specific difference. For example: "I'd prefer not to take part in the study, because if I did I'd miss the recreation period we have each day." (Note that the comparative clause "which won't be the case if I decline to participate" can be inferred from the subject's explanation.)

1   Subject makes comparison statement, but does not include a statement of a specific consequence. For example, "It will be better if I stay out of the study."

0   Subject makes no comparative statements.

> ### *Subpart 3*
> ### *Generating Consequences*

Rating   Guidelines

2   Subject must give at least two reasonable everyday consequences, including at least one for each of the two inquiry questions.

Note: Everyday consequences must go beyond those in the disclosure, and must refer to practical everyday activities or social relationships. For example, if the study involves venipuncture, "My arm may hurt" is not sufficient; "I won't be able to play in my bowling league if my arm hurts" is sufficient.

1   Subject gives one or more reasonable everyday consequences for one of the inquiry questions, but none for the other.

0   Subject gives no reasonable everyday consequences, even with adequate encouragement.

> ### *Subpart 4*
> ### *Logical Consistency*

Rating   Guidelines

2   Subject's final choice (in Expressing a Choice) follows logically from the subject's own reasoning, as explained by the subject in response to the three previous subparts.

Rating	Guidelines

1   It is not clear whether the choice follows logically from the subject's own reasoning.

0   Subject's choice clearly does not follow logically from subject's own reasoning.

Reasoning Summary Ratings

Add the ratings from the four Reasoning sections to obtain a Reasoning Summary Rating, which will be between 0 and 8.

─────── | Expressing a Choice | ───────

There is only one item in this section.

Rating	Guidelines

2   Subject states a choice

1   Subject states more than one choice, seems ambivalent.

0   Subject does not state a choice.

REFERENCES

Appelbaum, P. S., & Grisso, T. (1988). Assessing patients' capacities to consent to treatment. *New England Journal of Medicine, 319,* 1635-1638.

Appelbaum, P. S., & Grisso, T. (1995). The MacArthur Treatment Competence Study, I: Mental illness and competence to consent to treatment. *Law and Human Behavior, 19,* 105-126.

Appelbaum, P. S., Grisso, T., Frank, E., O'Donnell, S., & Kupfer, D. (1999). Competence of depressed patients for consent to research. *American Journal of Psychiatry, 156,* 1380-1384.

Appelbaum, P. S., & Roth, L. H. (1982). Competency to consent to research: A psychiatric overview. *Archives of General Psychiatry, 39,* 951-958.

Berg, J. W., & Appelbaum, P. S. (1999). Subjects' capacity to consent to neurobiological research. In H. A. Pincus, J. A. Lieberman, & S. Ferris (Eds.), *Ethics in Psychiatric Research: A Resource Manual for Human Subjects Protection* (pp. 81-106). Washington, DC: American Psychiatric Press.

Berg, J. W., Appelbaum, P. S., & Grisso T. (1996). Constructing competence: Formulating standards of legal competence to make medical decisions. *Rutgers Law Review, 48,* 345-396.

Berg, J. W., Appelbaum, P. S., Lidz, C. W., & Parker, L. (2001). *Informed Consent: Legal Theory and Clinical Practice* (2nd ed.). New York: Oxford University Press.

Carpenter, W. T., Gold, J. M., Lahti, A. C., Queern, C. A., Conley, R. R., Bartko, J. J., Kovnick, J., & Appelbaum, P. S. (2000). Decisional capacity for informed consent in schizophrenia research. *Archives of General Psychiatry, 57*, 533-538.

Grisso, T., & Appelbaum, P. S. (1998a). *Assessing Competence to Consent to Treatment: A Guide for Physicians and Other Health Professionals*. New York: Oxford University Press.

Grisso, T., & Appelbaum, P. S. (1998b). *MacArthur Competence Assessment Tool for Treatment (MacCAT-T)*. Sarasota, FL: Professional Resource Press.

Kim, S. Y. H., Caine, E. D., Currier, G. W., Leibovici, A., & Ryan, J. M. (2001). Assessing the competence of persons with Alzheimer's disease in providing informed consent for participation in research. *American Journal of Psychiatry, 158*, 712-717.

National Bioethics Advisory Commission. (1998). *Research Involving Persons With Mental Disorders That May Affect Decision-Making Capacity*. Rockville, MD: Author.

APPENDIX A

Sample MacCAT-CR
Interview

Sample MacCAT-CR Interview

This sample MacCAT-CR interview is designed to illustrate how the principles outlined in the MacCAT-CR manual can be operationalized in the context of a specific project. The hypothetical project chosen for illustrative purposes is a double-blind, placebo-controlled study of a new medication for schizophrenia.

Understanding

U-1 Disclosure (Nature of project)—"You have been asked to be in a research project to see whether a new medication is effective. We are asking you because you have schizophrenia, the condition that the new medication is designed to treat. The project lasts for 6 weeks. During that time, each person in the project will have blood drawn every week. Every other day the person will be asked to answer a set of questions about how he or she is feeling."

"Do you have any questions about what I just said?"

"Can you tell me your understanding of what I just said?"

[Record responses in appropriate sections below]

a) *Purpose of project*
[If subject fails to mention spontaneously, ask: "What is the purpose of the research project I described to you?"]

b) *Duration of project* (Procedural element No. 1)
[If subject fails to mention spontaneously, ask: "How long will the research project last?"]

c) *Blood drawing* (Procedural element No. 2)
[If subject fails to mention spontaneously, ask: "What sorts of things will be done with people who agree to be in the study?"]

d) *Every-other-day interviews* (Procedural element No. 3)
[If subject fails to mention spontaneously, ask: "What else will be done with people who agree to be in the study?"]

U-2 Disclosure (Primary purpose is research, not individualized care)—"It is important for you to understand that the project in which you have been asked to participate is a research project. That means its main purpose is to help the doctors figure out whether the new medication can help some people with schizophrenia. The main purpose is not to find out whether it works for the people in the study, as it would be if this were ordinary treatment."

"Do you have any questions about what I just said?"

"Can you tell me your understanding of what I just said?"

[Record answer below.]

[If subject fails to mention spontaneously, ask: "What is the main purpose of what the doctors are trying to do in this study?"]

U-3 Disclosure (Effect of research methods on individualized care)— "Because this is a research project, not ordinary treatment, the doctors will be doing things that they would not do in ordinary hospitals/ clinics, like those where you may have been treated before. For example, some people who are in this project will get the new medication, but others will get a sugar pill instead—a pill with no medicine in it (called a placebo). Whether they get the new medication or the sugar pill will be decided by chance. Neither the doctors nor the subjects will know whether they are getting the new medication or the sugar pill. All these things are done to see whether the new medication is better than no medication at all."

"Do you have any questions about what I just said?"

"Can you tell me your understanding of what I just said?"

[Record responses in appropriate sections below.]

a) *Placebo*
   [If subject fails to mention spontaneously, ask: "Will all people in the project get the new medication?"]

b) *Randomized assignment*
   [If subject fails to mention spontaneously, ask: "How will it be determined what kind of pills each of the people in the project will receive?"]

c) *Double blind*
   [If subject fails to mention spontaneously, ask: "Who will know what kind of pill each of the people in the study is receiving?"]

U-4a Disclosure (Benefits of participation)—"There are several benefits that could result if people agree to be in this project. First, the doctors will know whether the new medication really does work for people with schizophrenia. Second, those people in the project who actually get the new medication may find out whether it works for them."

"Do you have any questions about what I just said?"

"Can you tell me your understanding of what I just said?"

[Record responses in appropriate sections below.]

a) *Societal benefit*
   [If subject fails to mention spontaneously, ask: "What might doctors learn about the treatment of schizophrenia if people decide to be in this research project?"]

b) *Personal benefit*
   [If subject fails to mention spontaneously, ask: "In what way might people who volunteer be better off by being in this research project?"]

U-4b Disclosure (Risks/Discomforts of participation)—"There are also several risks and discomforts to which people who are in this study will be exposed. First, the new medication can cause twitching muscles in some people. Second, all people in the study will have two tubes of blood taken from a vein in their arm each week of the project."

"Do you have any questions about what I just said?"

"Can you tell me your understanding of what I just said?"

[Record responses in appropriate sections below.]

a) *Muscle spasms*
   [If subject fails to mention spontaneously, ask: "What unpleasant effects can the medication cause in some people?"]

b) *Blood drawing*
   [If subject fails to mention spontaneously, ask: "What uncomfortable things will have to be done to people in the study?"]

U-5 Disclosure (Ability to withdraw/receive ordinary care)—"No one has to be in this study. People who agree to be in this research project can change their minds at any time. If they don't agree to be in this study or if they decide to stop, they will be referred to the Outpatient Clinic for the usual treatment for schizophrenia."

"Do you have any questions about what I just said?"

"Can you tell me your understanding of what I just told you?"

[Record responses below.]

[If subject fails to mention spontaneously, ask: "What will happen if a person refuses to be in the research project, or decides to stop once it begins?"]

Appreciation

A-1 (Subject believes that his or her personal benefits are not the primary objective of the study)—"Do you believe that you have been asked to be in this study primarily for your personal benefit?"

Then ask: "What makes you believe that this (was/wasn't) the reason you were asked?"

[Record responses below.]

A-2 (Subject believes that there is a reasonable possibility that being in the experimental condition may be less personally beneficial)—"Do you believe that you could get the sugar pill?"

Then ask: "What makes you believe that this (could/couldn't) happen in your case?"

[Record responses below.]

A-3 (Subject believes that a personal decision to decline/withdraw will be honored)—"What do you believe would happen if you were to decide not to be in this study?"

Then ask: "What makes you believe that this would happen?"

[Record responses below.]

Expressing a Choice

"As you know, you have been invited to participate in a research project testing a new medication for the treatment of schizophrenia. Do you think you are more likely to want to participate or not to want to participate?"

[Record choice below.]

```
┌─────────────────────────────────┐
│  ┌───────────────────────────┐  │
│  │        Reasoning          │  │
│  └───────────────────────────┘  │
└─────────────────────────────────┘
```

R-1/R-2 (Consequential and comparative reasoning)—"You think that you are more likely to want (insert subject's choice) in the study. Tell me what it is that makes that option better than the other."

[Record explanation below. Probe to explore reasoning process.]

R-3 (Generating consequences)—"I told you about some of the possible benefits and risks or discomforts of participating in the research project. The benefits are that those subjects who actually get the new medication may find out whether it works for them. The risks and discomforts are that the new medications can cause twitching muscles in some people, and all people in the study will have two tubes of blood taken from a vein in their arm each week. What are some ways that these could affect (could have affected) your everyday activities if you participate (had participated) in the research project?"

[Record responses below.]

[If the subject fails to mention a consequence of either the benefits or the risks/discomforts, ask: "How might (restate benefit or risk) affect your everyday life?"]

Final Choice

"A few minutes ago you told me that you favored participating/not participating in the research project. What do you think now that we have discussed everything? What do you want to do?"

[Record choice below.]

Reasoning

R-4 (Logical consistency of choice)—[Interviewer records and explains presence or absence of logical consistency in subject's choice.]

APPENDIX B

MacCAT-CR
Record Form

MacCAT-CR Record Form

Subject: _____   Interviewer: _____

Record ID#: _____   Date: _____

_____

Understanding (Each item is rated 0-2)

1. Nature of project
   a) _____
   b) _____
   c) _____
   d) _____   Subtotal: [   ]

2. Primary purpose
   is research.   Subtotal: [   ]

3. Effects on
   individualized care
   a) _____
   b) _____
   c) _____   Subtotal: [   ]

4. Benefits and risks/
   discomforts
   a) _____
   b) _____
   c) _____
   d) _____   Subtotal: [   ]

5. Ability to
   withdraw   Subtotal: [   ]

TOTAL Understanding Score (0-26): [   ]

Appreciation (Each item is rated 0-2)

1. Object not personal benefit

2. Possibility of reduced benefit

3. Withdrawal possible

TOTAL Appreciation Score (0-6):

Reasoning (Each item is rated 0-2)

1. Consequential reasoning

2. Comparative reasoning

3. Generating consequences

3. Logical consistency of choice

TOTAL Reasoning Score (0-8):

Expressing a Choice (Rate 0-2):

TOTAL Expressing a Choice Score (0-2):

APPENDIX C

Subjects' Capacity to Consent to Neurobiological Research*

Jessica Wilen Berg, JD, and
Paul S. Appelbaum, MD

*Note. From *Ethics in Psychiatric Research: A Resource Manual for Human Subjects Protection* (pp. 81-106), by H. A. Pincus, J. A. Lieberman, and S. Ferris, 1999, Washington, DC: American Psychiatric Press. Copyright © 1999 by the American Psychiatric Publishing, Inc. Reprinted with permission.

Persons' capacity to make health care decisions has become a popular topic of discussion among physicians, lawyers, philosophers, and researchers. The increased interest in capacity was prompted by changes in informed consent law over the last 40 years. Historically, physicians rarely sought informed consent from patients and frequently disclosed to patients neither the nature of their disorder nor the intended course of treatment. Thus patients' capacity to make health care decisions was usually unimportant. In fact, the previously common decision-making model stemmed from the idea that all patients were per se incompetent to make medical decisions (because they lacked medical training) and therefore such choices should be left to experts (i.e., medical professionals).

One of the first American cases to speak of a consent requirement rejected the notion that patients should not be allowed control over their medical care and noted that "every human being of adult years and sound mind has a right to determine what shall be done with his body" (*Schloendorff v. Society of New York Hospital* 1914). The case emphasized the concept of voluntary consent; that is, the patient must freely give permission for a specific procedure to occur. Although a person not of "sound mind" was presumed unable to consent, most cases during this period focused simply on whether the patient did or did not consent, regardless of the competence of that consent. The current view of informed consent in this country began with a trio of cases in the late 1950s and early 1960s. The first of these, *Salgo v. Leland Stanford Junior University Board of Trustees* (1957), coined the term *informed consent* and held not only that patients must freely consent but also that they must be fully informed by practitioners about treatment options. It was this information requirement that prompted increased scrutiny of patient capacity—if a patient is not able to understand the information disclosed, he or she should not be considered competent to consent.

Today valid informed consent requires that a patient be given sufficient relevant facts; be free from coercion, undue influence, and unfair manipulation; and be competent to make a decision. *Competence* is used here to mean that individuals have sufficient cognitive capacities to reach decisions in a rational fashion.* This element of a valid consent derives from the view that some minimal degree of rationality in decision making is required if individual interests are to be protected; otherwise, decisions with regard to the interests of the person essentially will be random. Thus competence, like the other informed consent requirements, is linked to autonomy—a competent person is one who is able to make decisions autonomously, or in accordance with his or her preferences (Morreim 1991). This element of informed consent is our focus.

About the same time as the legal doctrine of informed consent to medical treatment was evolving, the doctrine of informed consent to research (prompted by the Nuremberg Code) gained attention. Historical abuses in medical experimentation (e.g., Nazi experiments during World War II, the Tuskegee syphilis experiments, and the Willowbrook hepatitis experiments) resulted in the promulgation of a series of ethical codes constraining biomedical research. Inspired by concern that human subjects not be misused, federal regulations and common law have combined to ensure that informed consent requirements are fully applicable to research (Appelbaum et al. 1987a; Department of Health and Human Services 1991; National Commission 1978). According to the current guidelines of the Department of Health and Human Services, "no investigator may involve a human being as a subject in research . . . unless the investigator has obtained the legally

---

*It is important to note that *competence* is a legal construct—in most jurisdictions only a court can decide whether a person is incompetent. Assessments of *capacity*, on the other hand, are left in the hands of medical or mental health professionals. We use the terms interchangeably, and unless otherwise specified, we are referring to clinical assessments of capacity, not legal determinations of competence.

effective consent of the subject or the subject's legally authorized representative" (§46.116). Although the regulations set forth specific disclosure requirements, as well as additional protections for vulnerable populations to ensure voluntary consent, they do not address the requirements for subject capacity. Moreover, cases and statutes that articulate standards of decision-making competence (all of them in the treatment arena) often lack sufficient explanation of both the terms used (such as *rationality*) and the mechanisms for applying the standards (Berg et al. 1996). As a result, investigators have had little guidance in regard to assessments of the decision-making competence of potential research subjects (Appelbaum 1997).

In this chapter we set forth a framework for thinking about the capacities involved in medical decision making, including decisions about research participation. Using this framework, we then examine empirical studies relating to the capacity of subjects to consent to neurobiological research and the implications of these studies for policy-related questions. Finally, we provide practical guidance for investigators engaged in research that involves cognitively impaired subjects.

CAPACITY TO CONSENT TO RESEARCH

Issues related to competence present particular problems for neurobiological researchers (Shamoo and Irving 1993). Many of the target subjects of such research have disorders that impair the very cognitive faculties on which they must rely to decide whether to participate in research. Concerns about capacity thus arise in several subject populations, including persons with mental illness (Elliott 1997); AIDS patients (Marks et al. 1992); elderly persons (Cassel 1988), especially those with dementia such as Alzheimer's disease (High et al. 1994); people with organic brain damage; and people with substance abuse problems. The National Institute of Mental Health's Epidemiologic

Catchment Area (ECA) study estimates that during the course of 1 year 2.7% of the adult population (or 4,293,000 people) has severe cognitive impairments (Regier et al. 1993). These disorders may render some proportion of potential subjects incompetent to consent to research, requiring that they not be entered into studies (even if they appear to be agreeing to participate) or that alternative mechanisms for authorizing their participation be developed (Berg 1996). To evaluate the capacity of these and other potential subjects to consent to research, standards of competence must be established.

The following discussion draws on standards of competence articulated in legal, medical, psychological, and ethical literature related to patient capacity to make treatment decisions. Several reasons are cited for applying the standards developed for competence to consent to treatment to decision making related to research. First, many research projects involve administration of treatment; in such cases, the tasks of deciding about treatment acceptance and research participation are intertwined. Second, the legal standards elaborated for competence to consent to treatment are closely related to standards for other decision-making tasks, such as making contracts (White and Denise 1991), writing wills, giving gifts, and even making decisions related to criminal defense (Bonnie 1993). Third, when we turn from the legal literature to medical, psychological, and bioethical writings, we find a similar approach: commentators do not distinguish between competence to consent to treatment and competence to consent to research (Appelbaum and Roth 1982). Although the types of information that the physician and the investigator must disclose may differ, and different procedures may be necessary to avoid infringing on persons' voluntary choice, the capacities needed to make a meaningful decision are much the same.

Standards for Determining Decision-Making Competence

Drawing on earlier work by Roth et al. (1977; Appelbaum & Roth 1982), Drs. Paul Appelbaum and Thomas Grisso have developed a framework of four standards that can stand alone or serve as components of an overall standard of competence: 1) ability to communicate a choice, 2) ability to understand relevant information, 3) ability to appreciate the nature of the situation and its likely consequences, and 4) ability to manipulate information rationally (Appelbaum and Grisso 1988). These standards are reflected in, and in fact drawn from, the law (Berg et al. 1996). Moreover, many commentators evince general agreement about the standards, although they may disagree about which standard should be applied in a specific situation (Berg et al. 1996). Each of the four elements is discussed in more detail in the following section.

Ability to communicate a choice is the least stringent standard applied by courts and legislatures. Potential subjects fail this test because of inability to either reach a decision (i.e., a patient simply cannot make up his or her mind or vacillates to such a degree that it is impossible to implement a choice) or effectively make known their wishes regarding research. Many courts use this standard as a threshold determination of competence, on the assumption that a person who cannot reach a decision or make that decision known to the outside world ought not to be afforded the power to guide his or her own affairs. Although ability to communicate a choice may be a necessary component of competence, it is not in itself sufficient: a person who can communicate a choice does not necessarily have the capacity to make a choice autonomously. Thus, many courts and commentators combine this standard with one or more of the others. Comatose, mute catatonic, or severely depressed persons, individuals with manic or catatonic excitements, and persons with severe psychotic thought disorders or severe dementia fall into this category.

Ms. A has chronic undifferentiated schizophrenia. When she initially is approached regarding participation in a new protocol designed to test the effect of her present medication on eating habits, she is enthusiastic. She appears to understand all of the implications of the study and consents to participation. Later that day, when the research assistant approaches Ms. A, she refuses to participate. Over the course of the next few days Ms. A repeatedly alternates between agreeing and refusing to participate. Because Ms. A is unable to make up her mind for a period of time long enough to allow the research to proceed, she should not be included in the study.

Mr. B has been admitted to a hospital for an acute psychotic episode. Unfortunately, the level of medication necessary to control his symptoms leaves him almost completely sedated. If the dose of medication is lowered, however, he rapidly reverts to a severe state of psychotic disorganization and disorientation. In neither his unmedicated psychotic nor his sedated state is Mr. B able to interact with people. Because he cannot communicate, he does not have the capacity to consent to research participation at this time.

The second and most common standard—*ability to understand relevant information*—focuses on the patient's comprehension of information related to the decision. *Understanding*, in this sense, is defined simply as the ability to comprehend the concepts involved in the informed consent disclosure; it does not necessarily include the ability to relate that information to the situation at hand. Thus a person may understand the information, but unless he or she can retain the information long enough for a decision to be made, he or she is not competent to consent. Impairments of intelligence, attention, and memory, whether due to organic or functional disorders, can affect this ability.

Mr. C has Wernicke-Korsakoff syndrome. Although he is able to take care of his daily needs, his short-term memory is almost nonexistent. When approached by a research assistant regarding participation in a long-term protocol, Mr. C appears to understand and is at first eager to help. However, after the research assistant has completed the informed consent disclosure, Mr. C has no recollection of anything that has been explained to him. A few minutes later, he does not even remember meeting the research assistant. Mr. C does not have the capacity to consent.

Ms. D is severely mentally retarded and lives in an institution. She can communicate with her caretaker on a rudimentary level but is unable to engage in higher-level discourse. When asked to do something that she does not like, she becomes agitated and resistant. Ms. D is approached by a graduate student at the institution and asked to participate in a study of behavioral reinforcements that would involve restricting her usual access to food. She indicates her understanding of the graduate student's instructions by her compliance with them. When the student attempts to assess her understanding of the experiment, however, Ms. D demonstrates no comprehension of the research. Thus, despite her compliance with the graduate student's instructions, Ms. D does not have the capacity to consent.

Ms. E is in the midst of an acute manic episode. She is constantly active, and her attention span usually lasts no more than a minute. A research assistant has tried a number of times to explain what is involved in a particular protocol. Each time, Ms. E interrupts any explanation within a couple of minutes, saying that she is willing to do whatever the doctor wants and then immediately launches into a monologue on a different subject. Ms. E does not have the capacity to consent.

The third standard, *ability to appreciate the nature of the situation and its likely consequences*, requires that the subject be able to apply abstractly understood information to his or her own situation. Therefore, this standard is often combined with an understanding requirement. Persons who understand that their physician believes they are ill but in the face of evidence that would persuade a reasonable person deny that this is so would not meet this standard. Denial (often called "lack of insight"), delusions, and psychotic levels of distortion can impair appreciation of the nature of the situation.

Mr. F has paranoid schizophrenia. He is college educated, well-read, and extremely intelligent. When approached by a research assistant regarding participation in a protocol, he is able to comprehend all of the information regarding the study, including the scientific basis for the experiment. He explains to the assistant that he knows that the physicians in the hospital are planning to kill him and that the research assistant is a covert agent sent to secret him away under cover of the research. Mr. F does not have the capacity to consent.

The fourth and final standard is the *ability to manipulate information rationally*. It focuses on reasoning capacity and addresses a person's ability to employ logical thought processes to compare the risks and benefits of treatment options. This standard does not look at the outcome of a decision but, like the understanding and appreciation elements, is concerned with the decision-making process. Thus, a person who can understand, appreciate, and communicate a decision may still be impaired if he or she is unable to process information logically, in accordance with his or her preferences. Conversely, a person may employ logical thought processes but base them on impaired understanding or appreciation.

Ms. G is 84 years old and has multi-infarct dementia. She is asked to participate in a drug trial for a new medication that may slow the progress of her disease. She is told that the study has a small chance (20%) of benefiting her personally, but given the advanced state of her vascular disease it probably will not increase her predicted life span. She tells the research assistant that she is very excited about this protocol because the 20% potential for benefit is much better than the 80% probability of no benefit that was explained to her with respect to a previous drug protocol. When the assistant questions this reasoning, he discovers that Ms. G lacks the ability to compare the risks and benefits of different alternatives. Because of this deficit in probabilistic reasoning skills, Ms. G may not have the capacity to consent. Efforts will now be made to teach her about relative risks, after which her reasoning ability will be retested.

Mr. H, who has AIDS-related dementia, is approached by a research assistant regarding participation in a drug trial. The protocol involves almost no chance of direct therapeutic benefit and a moderate degree of risk, and it requires the subject to remain at the study site for the duration of the experiment

(6 weeks). Mr. H has made it clear throughout his illness that he would like to move to a home care situation. Moreover, he has stated more than once that he has accepted that there is nothing that can be done to cure his illness and thus he would rather spend what time he has left with his family. When he consents to participate in the study, his primary care physician is concerned that the reasoning behind his choice is not consistent with his expressed desire to go home. Further inquiry is required regarding the basis for his choice and his ability to consent to research participation.

Empirical Studies of Decision-Making Capacity

Several empirical studies have examined how well persons perform on these standards of decision-making competence. Most of the findings on decision-making performance are from studies of consent to treatment, not consent to research (Appelbaum and Grisso 1995). However, these findings have important implications for research decision making. For example, the recent MacArthur Treatment Competence Study compared the capacity to make treatment decisions of newly hospitalized patients with schizophrenia, major depression, and angina pectoris with the capacity of community control subjects matched for age, gender, race, education, and occupation (Appelbaum and Grisso 1995; Grisso and Appelbaum 1995; Grisso et al. 1995). Because the study looked at both patients hospitalized with mental illness and patients hospitalized with medical illness,* it enabled the investigators to examine the effect of mental illness per se (as opposed to the undifferentiated effects of hospitalization) on decision-making abilities. Moreover, the researchers were able to draw conclusions about the decision-making capacity of medically ill persons, and this infor-

---

*Mental illnesses are medical illnesses, but for clarification we separate the two here.

mation can be used as a standard against which to examine decision making by impaired populations. If subjects who have illnesses that commonly result in cognitive impairments do no worse on measures of decision-making capacity than medically ill subjects, there is less need for investigators to implement special precautions when engaging in research with these groups. This finding does not, of course, mean that no protections should be instituted. If subjects in general (regardless of type of illness) show impairments of decision-making capacity, a prudent researcher should take steps to ensure that competent decision making occurs.

Neurobiological researchers are likely to be most concerned about the abilities of subjects who have disorders that make them candidates for research participation but whose illnesses often result in cognitive impairment. It is these groups—for example, persons with mental illness and elderly persons (especially those with some form of dementia)—on whom we focus here. Although researchers have undertaken numerous studies on the neuropsychological performance of substance abusers, and on the effects of alcohol-induced impairments, we could find no empirical studies of the capacity of substance abusers to consent to research participation or to make treatment decisions. Nevertheless, a recent paper by the College on Problems of Drug Dependence (1995) expressed concern about the capacity of substance abusers to assess objectively the risks inherent in research. Similarly, Kleber (1989) noted that drug use can affect subject comprehension and lead individuals to overestimate their ability to deal with the experimental procedure; Kleber concluded that informed consent should therefore be acquired only when the investigator is certain that subject is no longer intoxicated. Because of the lack of empirical studies involving this population, we focus primarily on data from elderly and psychiatric populations, bearing in mind that substance abusers probably present many of the same issues. Indeed, the high incidence of HIV and mental illness in this population may result in an even greater percentage of cognitively impaired subjects than in elderly and psychiatric populations.

Individuals who fail to meet the first standard (communication) are the least problematic from the perspective of neurobiological researchers: potential subjects' inability to offer consent will be evident and consent will be sought elsewhere or subjects will be excluded from the study. Thus, here we address only potential subjects' ability to understand, appreciate, and reason.

Understanding. Although a number of studies have explored psychiatric subjects' ability to consent to research, many of the early investigations neglected to ascertain whether the appropriate information had been communicated to subjects (Riecken and Ravich 1982). Thus, it is difficult to know whether poor performance was a result of cognitive deficits or inadequate disclosure. Not all studies have suffered from this flaw, however, and those that examined understanding after controlled information disclosure found that significant numbers of individuals with cognitive impairments had substantial difficulty understanding disclosed information. For example, the MacArthur study examined hospitalized angina patients' understanding of 1) the nature of the disorder, 2) the nature of the treatment being recommended, 3) the probable benefits of the treatment, 4) the probable risks and discomforts of the treatment, and 5) the relevant benefits and risks of an alternative treatment; researchers then compared angina patients' understanding with that of schizophrenia patients and community control subjects. Subjects with schizophrenia did significantly worse than subjects with angina or community control subjects when tested on a measure of understanding: 28% fell in the impaired range compared with 7.4% of angina patients and 2.4% of control subjects. (Impaired subjects were defined as those who, after comparison with everyone else, scored in the bottom 5% of the distribution of scores for the total study sample.) Depressed subjects, on the other hand, performed no differently than medically ill subjects or non-ill control subjects (5.4% scored in the impaired range).

Two studies by Loren Roth and his colleagues in the early 1980s examined psychiatric patients' decision making in the research rather than treatment context. In the first study, 41 patients with affective disorders (of whom only 5 were psychotic) were asked to participate in a study of their electroencephalogram patterns during sleep (Roth et al. 1982). Approximately one-quarter of the subjects understood half or less of the disclosed information, and a mere 5% understood 87% or more of the information. Of the 19 subjects whose consent discussions were videotaped, 4 were rated as probably incompetent by independent judges. The second study (Benson et al. 1988) examined the understanding of 88 psychiatric patients recruited to participate in four research projects. Data analysis revealed that

> while prospective research subjects generally demonstrated good understanding of the purpose of the written consent form and their right to refuse or withdraw from the study . . . they frequently did not understand the psychiatric research project's purpose, or why they had been asked to participate in it. Subjects also often demonstrated poor understanding of important methodological aspects of the study, including the randomized and double-blind treatment assignment. (p. 469)

These findings suggest that how well we rate the ability of psychiatric patients to understand information in research settings depends on what types of information we consider it important for them to comprehend. The Benson et al. study also found that patients with schizophrenia and those with high levels of psychopathology (measured by the Brief Psychiatric Rating Scale [Overall and Gorham 1962]) performed more poorly than patients with borderline personality disorder and subjects who were generally less impaired.

Studies of elderly subjects have shown similar difficulties in understanding. Fitten and Waite's 1990 study of decision-making capacity in elderly persons found that while healthy elderly individuals showed little or no impairment of understanding ability, hospitalized medically ill patients (who were neurologically and psychiatrically intact) "failed to substantially understand key issues in treatment despite language and form simplification of consent documents" (p. 1720). Stanley and colleagues (1984) used a series of hypothetical research studies to assess the capacity of medical patients to consent to research. They found that elderly patients demonstrated poorer comprehension of consent information than younger patients. These findings are consistent with studies of understanding in treatment settings in which elderly patients were less able to remember information and less able to understand consent forms (Stanley et al. 1988).

These deficiencies in understanding, however, may be remedied. For example, a study testing the effect of different disclosure formats on the understanding and reasoning capacity of elderly residents in a long-term care facility found that comprehension was significantly better when the information was presented in a simplified or storybook format (Tymchuk et al. 1988). A more serious problem is the high incidence of dementia in this subject population, which may result in permanent impairment of decision-making capacity (Speer 1990). One estimate suggests that approximately 6% of individuals over age 65 have severe dementia, and an additional 10%-15% have mild to moderate cognitive impairment (Cummings and Benson 1992). Another study has estimated that the incidence of Alzheimer's disease in persons over age 65 is 10% (Evans et al. 1989).

A study by Sachs et al. (1994) examined the willingness of persons with dementia to participate in four hypothetical research protocols. Interviewers judged subject capacity based on subjective evaluation of the consistency and quality of responses related to why subjects would or would not participate. They found that persons with dementia were less able than the well elderly to give cogent reasons for their decisions and were less able to identify specific risks and benefits. Preliminary results in another study of treatment decision making by patients with Alzheimer's disease showed that elderly control subjects without Alzheimer's disease performed significantly better than both mild and moderate Alzheimer's disease patients on measures of understanding (Marson et al. 1994). Moreover, the mildly ill patients performed significantly better than the moderately ill group, providing support for the notion that greater severity of illness leads to greater impairment in decision-making capacity.

Appreciation. The ability to appreciate the nature of a situation and its likely consequences has been the subject of extensive exploration in psychiatric populations because of its close connection to core symptoms of mental disorders. Diminished ability to appreciate that one is ill has been found to be the key diagnostic feature of schizophrenia in two multinational studies (Carpenter et al. 1976; Wilson et al. 1986). In addition, patients with schizophrenia or severe depression may be impaired in their ability to appreciate the potential value of treatment. The MacArthur Treatment Competence Study found that subjects with schizophrenia were more likely to deny completely the presence of illness than were depressed patients (35% versus 4%), although similar proportions of both groups denied the potential for effective treatment (13% versus 14%). On a composite measure of appreciation of the presence of illness and the potential for treatment, a total of 22.6% of subjects with schizophrenia scored in the impaired decision-making range compared with 11.9% of depressed subjects and 4.8% of angina subjects. (This measure was not administered to non-ill control subjects.)

Appreciation problems have been clearly demonstrated in connection with consent to research. Potential subjects with psychiatric disorders often fail to appreciate the nature of the research and its potential impact on their treatment. One recurring problem is the prevalence of therapeutic misconception (Appelbaum et al. 1987b). A study of psychiatric patients found that many of them misconstrued the nature of the research they were involved in and erroneously believed that they would be receiving the treatment their doctors thought was best for their condition (Appelbaum et al. 1982). More specifically, the study found that schizophrenia and depressed subjects involved in a double-blind experiment were unaware that they would be assigned randomly to different drug regimens and that the researchers would not know which drug they were taking. Therapeutic misconception is not limited to psychiatric patients, however. A study of patients undergoing randomized clinical trials for the treatment of cancer found that a significant number had difficulty distinguishing between the treatment and research components of the protocol and more than half failed to understand an explicit explanation of randomization (Simes et al. 1986).

Sachs et al. (1994) noted that the inability of most dementia patients to recognize that they have a memory problem provides one explanation for why such individuals fail most competence standards. The Marson et al. study (1994, p. 13) that examined treatment decision making of Alzheimer's disease patients specifically looked at patients' "capacity to 'appreciate' the emotional and cognitive consequences of a choice." Consistent with the study by Sachs et al., this study found that patients with mild Alzheimer's disease performed significantly better than patients with moderate Alzheimer's disease, and control subjects without Alzheimer's disease performed better than both groups of ill patients.

Reasoning. Few studies of persons' ability to manipulate information rationally have been undertaken, and they often rely on paradigms that bear little resemblance to decision making in clinical or research contexts. For example, one study employed a gambling paradigm to measure the ability of patients with schizophrenia to weigh risks, benefits, and probabilities in an internally consistent manner (Rosenfeld et al. 1992). The study found that involuntarily committed inpatients with chronic schizophrenia were significantly less able to consistently weigh risks, benefits, and probabilities than chronic schizophrenia outpatients and nonpatient family control subjects.

The MacArthur Treatment Competence Study examined the degree to which subjects demonstrated an ability to 1) seek information, 2) consider the consequences of treatment alternatives, 3) compare two treatment alternatives, 4) consider a number of treatment alternatives at one time, 5) generate potential real-life consequences of the disclosed risks or discomforts of the treatment, 6) consistently apply personal preferences, 7) make logical inferences about ordinal relationships (i.e., A > B, B > C, choose the largest), and 8) distinguish correctly the relative values of numerical probabilities. The study found that subjects with schizophrenia or severe depression performed significantly worse than angina subjects and community control subjects. In percentage terms, 24% of schizophrenia subjects, 7.6% of depressed subjects, 0% of angina subjects, and 2% of control subjects fell into the impaired range. Impaired performance by schizophrenia patients on this and other measures of capacity (understanding and appreciation) was positively correlated with conceptual disorganization, unusual or delusional thought content, and, to a lesser extent, hallucinations.

If one takes decision outcome as a proxy for rationality of decision process, three studies of research decision making by Barbara Stanley and colleagues also are relevant here. Looking at a group of psychiatric patients with mixed diagnoses who were asked whether they would participate in hypothetical research projects, Stanley et al. (1982) found that 40% of acutely hospitalized patients said they would agree to take part in high-risk/low-benefit projects, whereas up to 32% refused low-risk/high-benefit participation. Although this finding suggests poor performance in the weighing of risks and benefits, a similar study that compared psychiatric and medical inpatients found no difference between the groups in willingness to participate in studies of either high or low risk (Stanley et al. 1981). Decision outcome is thus probably not a very good proxy for reasoning ability. Stanley et al. (1984) also found that although a significantly greater proportion of elderly than younger patients agreed to participate in a high-risk/low-benefit study, there was no overall difference in the quality of reasoning of elderly and younger medical patients. Although their age may not pose a problem per se, elderly patients who have dementia may demonstrate greater impairment of reasoning ability. For example, Marson et al. (1994) found that subjects with either mild or moderate Alzheimer's disease performed significantly worse than non-ill control subjects on a test of rational thinking (with the mild group performing better than the moderate group).

GUIDANCE FOR POLICY MAKERS

What are the implications of these findings for research involving subjects with cognitive impairments? First, although specific concerns can be identified, broad generalizations should be avoided. It cannot reasonably be maintained that psychiatric patients or elderly patients as a class are incompetent to offer (or refuse) their informed consent for participation in research. Many of these people, perhaps most, retain decision-making abilities indistinguishable from those found in the general population. However, it cannot be argued that decisional incompetence is simply not a problem among these populations. On the contrary, substantial impairment is not uncommon. Thus, researchers need to be especially sensitive to the possible difficulties in obtaining informed consent from people with severe mental illness, elderly persons (especially those with some form of dementia), and people with substance abuse problems.

Second, because cognitive impairment varies in degree, problems may range from mild difficulties in understanding consent documents to severe incapacity rendering the subject incompetent to make any research decision. Although diagnosis cannot generally be used as a means of classifying incompetent subjects, different groups of cognitively impaired subjects may present different issues for investigators. Many people with mental illness (and substance abusers), for example, have intermittent periods of increased capacity. As a result, although certain types of experimentation may be impermissible at one time, they may be possible at another, either when the individual is competent to give his or her own consent or through the use of advance directives or instructions to a proxy in anticipation of later relapse. Other people, such as those with Alzheimer's disease or AIDS, are likely to become more impaired as the research progresses. Therefore, it is important to discuss all aspects of the research (including future involvement) with the subject during the early stages of the illness.

Mr. I is a long-time substance abuser. He has been drug free for 2 months. However, in the past he has failed to remain drug free for long periods of time. He has recently started using phencyclidine (PCP) again when he is approached by a research assistant, who is unaware that Mr. I is no longer drug free. Although Mr. I consents to participate in the research, over the next few days the assistant notices that the subject's behavior becomes increasingly erratic and that he has developed delusions about the research project. Mr. I no longer has the capacity to consent and should not be included in the protocol. A few weeks later, at the urging of his wife, Mr. I is back in treatment and again drug free. At this time he may be asked again to consent to research participation.

Ms. J has recently discovered that she has Alzheimer's disease. Except for minor lapses in memory, she has not yet begun to show signs of the illness. Her physician asks her whether she would be interested in taking part in a long-term research protocol studying the progression of her illness. She indicates her willingness and includes her newly appointed proxy decision maker in the discussions regarding research participation. She makes it clear that the proxy is authorized to consent to her continued participation in the protocol even after she becomes incapacitated.

How, then, should policy makers react to the current concern that incompetent patients may be consenting to research participation in violation of the principles of informed consent and to their personal detriment? Whatever action is taken should be sensitive to the balance of interests involved. Protection of the rights and well-being of potential subjects is of great importance. So, too, however, is the advancement of knowledge of disorders affecting the brain. As we guard patients' rights and interests, the burden of additional protections on the conduct of research must also be taken into account. The real issue is not whether we can add enough safeguards (because another safeguard can usually be added) but rather whether the additional protection it provides is worth the potential negative impact on the advance of knowledge. In the end, we seek to achieve a balance between the need for new scientific knowledge to advance medical treatment and the protection of individual autonomy (Candilis et al. 1993).

With this issue in mind, we need to address problems related to competence to consent to research in three areas. First, we need a more precise formulation of the degree of capacity required for competent consent to research. Second, we need a means of identifying persons who may lack the requisite capacities. Third, we must develop approaches to compensate for decision-making impairment among potential research subjects, including mechanisms for more easily obtaining substituted consent when appropriate. Each of these problems is considered in the following sections.

Capacities Necessary

A standard for competence to make research decisions should result in the optimum proportions of people being correctly identified as competent and incompetent. That is, we should be as concerned about incorrectly labeling autonomous agents as incompetent as we are about labeling nonautonomous agents as competent. We must take into account a number of aspects of formulating a standard. Initially, the choice of components is important, because different standards may result in different people and different numbers of people being identified as impaired. Assuming, for our purposes, that all four components described previously (communication, understanding, appreciation, and reasoning) should be included in a standard of competence (Berg et al. 1996), the question remains where the cutoff points should be. That is, below what level of performance should we say that a person is not competent to give or withhold consent? This consideration breaks down into two issues. First, in addition to deciding to apply an understanding standard, we must also establish how much understanding is necessary in a quantitative sense: It is sufficient if a subject manifests understanding of only 50% of the disclosed information, or must a subject understand 95% of what he or she is told? Second, the necessary aspects of performance must be identified. For example, a subject may understand that the research in question will involve a comparison between people who actually get the experimental medium and control subjects who will get a placebo but fail to grasp that assignment to a group is random. Is understanding of both pieces of information necessary?

Demanding total comprehension and appreciation, along with high-level reasoning abilities, from subjects with cognitive impairments is unrealistic because most members of the general population would fail such tests. Comparisons with nonpatient groups, suitably matched, might provide a statistical basis for identifying levels of performance that fall so far below the general norm as to justify calling a person incompetent, but this approach, too, is likely to be unsatisfactory. A rigid cutoff of this sort fails to take into account the possibility, for example, that different levels of capacity may be required depending on the nature of the research project to which consent is being sought. Thus, instead of using a fixed level of competence, a sliding scale could be applied (Drane 1984; President's Commission 1982). This scale would allow competence determinations to take into account the features of the subject's situation, which many commentators believe is desirable. For example, a subject would be required to demonstrate both understanding and appreciation for all research decisions, but the level of understanding or appreciation required might vary depending on the specific context. A subject who showed minor impairments on the competence measures might be competent to make simple research decisions, but those same impairments would be of greater concern if the research decision involved more complex elements. Relevant factors to consider might include the complexity of the research protocol, the amount of risk entailed, and the potential for direct therapeutic benefit. For minimal risk research, unless substantial direct therapeutic benefit is possible, it may be reasonable to allow persons to make their own decisions, even in the face of considerable impairment, knowing that adverse consequences are unlikely to ensue whichever way they decide. As the risks of either participating or not participating rise, however, more demanding levels of capacity may be required (Berg 1996).

Mr. K is in his mid-50s and has mild dementia following a stroke. He is asked to participate in a study of lifestyle changes of early-onset stroke victims. After explaining how the study will be run and indicating that it involves little or no risk and has no potential for direct therapeutic benefit, the research assistant asks Mr. K whether he has any questions. Mr. K demonstrates comprehension of most of the information imparted (approximately 70%) and indicates that he is aware that he will derive no direct therapeutic benefit from the study. He is unclear, however, about why researchers would want to include him because he did not have a stroke. Nevertheless, he is willing to participate because he feels that medical research is important. Although Mr. K demonstrates somewhat impaired appreciation (he does not deny the symptoms of his dementia—including loss of memory and increased difficulty in understanding—just their origin), he probably has the capacity to participate in this low-risk study.

A few weeks later another investigator, hearing about Mr. K's willingness to participate in research, approaches him to ask whether he would be willing to participate in a drug trial. This protocol involves a significant degree of risk but also has a potential for direct therapeutic benefit. Mr. K's failure of appreciation may be of more concern here. If he cannot appreciate the potential therapeutic benefit (because he denies the stroke), he may lack the capacity to consent (because he cannot weigh the risks and benefits of participation). Moreover, Mr. K's difficulties in understanding are also a problem because this protocol involves higher risk.

As noted previously, reliance on quantitative data alone (e.g., how much the subject understands) to determine who lacks competence may be inappropriate, because certain aspects of understanding, appreciation, and rational manipulation may be so crucial to competent consent that we would not feel comfortable allowing a person to make a decision in their absence. A patient who scores above the cutoff point for impairment on a given measure (because he or she does not score in the lower range of the score distribution when compared with the rest of the population) arguably still should be considered incompetent if he or she is incapable of demonstrating a particular capacity that is essential for competent decision making. For example, a subject who is asked to enter a research protocol and understands the procedure in which he or she is asked to participate but fails to understand the distinction between ordinary treatment and research probably should be considered incompetent to consent to participate in the experiment.

To date, resolution of these issues has been left to the decentralized mechanisms we have developed for overseeing research. Institutional review boards (IRBs) may ask investigators to provide assurance that incompetent subjects will be excluded from participation, but they rarely (if ever) have specified how to define that population.

Moreover, investigators themselves may be untutored in the nuances of assessing competence, and they usually leave recruitment of subjects in the hands of research assistants. As a result, practices vary widely across research projects. Our inability to say definitively what level of capacity is required in any project makes it difficult to supervise investigators and unfair to criticize them for not following standards that may be formulated only after the fact. Were general standards developed, they would have to be flexible enough to allow application to a wide variety of research projects with very different patient populations. Although difficult, the task should not be impossible. Important considerations include which of the four components (communication, understanding, appreciation, or reasoning) should be made part of a standard of competence, what level of ability a subject must demonstrate to meet the standard, and to what the standard should be applied.

Identifying Impairments

Once clear criteria exist for determining whether potential subjects are competent to consent to research, it is necessary to develop means to identify persons who may lack the requisite capacities. The creation of generally agreed-upon criteria would permit the development of screening mechanisms to identify subjects at risk for incompetence. These screening methods might be based on clinical judgment, measures of psychopathology or dementia correlated with significant impairment (Berg et al. 1996; Schachter et al. 1994; Stanley et al. 1985), or tests aimed at consent-related abilities per se. For example, Appelbaum and Grisso have produced a condensed version of the MacArthur competence assessment instruments (the MacCAT-CR) for use in a research setting (see Sections I–III, pp. 5–25). Once reliable indicators of capacity are identified or developed, special training in the use of assessment instruments may be required for those engaged in subject recruitment. In some cases the assessment may be done by research assistants or clinicians, who are ordinarily involved in obtaining informed consent. In other cases, consent specialists who are trained to screen and obtain consent in different settings may be needed. Given the economic and time constraints of many protocols, a screening mechanism for research participation ideally should be easily administered (e.g., by research assistants) and adaptable to a number of different research projects.

Whether a screening mechanism should be used routinely to assess subjects' decision-making capacities depends on the cost of applying the procedure to the target population balanced against the benefit of identifying incompetent decision makers (assuming the screening mechanism is effective—that is, it appropriately identifies impaired or incompetent subjects). Three factors are crucial here: first, the cost of the screening depends on the method used; second, the degree of benefit depends on the prevalence of incapacity in the population, or the base rate; and third, benefits also depend on the extent of harm avoided.

For the general population, competence screening is probably unwarranted because the incidence of incapacity is relatively low. Thus, the likelihood that an incompetent person will be allowed to make a decision is correspondingly low. This likelihood is much higher, however, in populations with schizophrenia or Alzheimer's disease. Even for these groups, competence screening may not be economically feasible except for more severely ill people. Consequently, a maximally efficient screening process would focus only on subjects who are clearly thought disordered, delusional, or otherwise severely cognitively impaired. As the risk inherent in a decision increases, however (e.g., a high-risk research project involving subjects with schizophrenia or a study with an uncertain risk-benefit ratio involving subjects with Alzheimer's disease), so does the justification for routine screening.

The Role of IRBs

Although developing standards and screening mechanisms is basically a task for national policy makers, local IRBs could take a more active role in ensuring appropriate consent. For example, IRBs could specify what standard of competence should be used for a particular protocol and when a capacity screening mechanism is warranted. Furthermore, as part of the initial protocol approval process, IRBs could require investigators to provide information on the use of screening mechanisms. Alternatively, IRBs could actively oversee the consent process or perhaps view a random sample of consent interactions. In addition, IRBs could provide information on appropriate consent mechanisms for subjects who are found to lack decision-making capacity. For example, an IRB might draft a basic document explaining what is meant by *substituted judgment* or *best interests* and give examples of how substitute decision makers should apply the standards in specific cases. The IRB could also specify the level of certainty needed to make a decision: Is it sufficient if the proxy believes that the subject more than likely would have consented if he or she had been competent (> 50% likelihood), or should a higher degree of certainty be required (such as 75% or even 90%)? The level of certainty needed may vary depending on the decision in question—less certainty is needed for lower-risk studies and more certainty is needed for higher-risk studies (Berg 1996). In cases in which there is a concern that either subjects or proxies will not understand the experiment because of the complicated nature of the research, and there are high risks involved, the IRB might require that the investigators take additional steps to ensure comprehension, such as employing a neutral third-party educator. The extent of the protections required depend on the case, but IRBs can clearly take a more active role in this context (Berg 1996; Bonnie 1997; Keyserlingk et al. 1995).

PRACTICAL GUIDANCE FOR RESEARCHERS

Though we lack definitive answers to the questions outlined previously (i.e., where to draw the line for incompetence and how to reliably identify incompetent subjects), the following suggestions may provide investigators with techniques for dealing with these uncertainties. First, investigators need to be aware that there will be some percentage of incompetent individuals in most populations with severe mental illness or dementia. Protocols submitted to IRBs should openly acknowledge this possibility, and practical means for dealing with such subjects should be designed.

Second, investigators need to specify for their project what constitutes an acceptable level of capacity. Because there is not a clear legal standard of competence to apply in research situations, investigators should develop one for their specific research protocols. The standard should identify the key information that must be understood by a subject before allowing participation and the disabling impairments (such as failure to appreciate the difference between research and treatment or inability to demonstrate internally consistent reasoning supporting participation) that will bar subject involvement. Because the levels of understanding, appreciation, and reasoning abilities required may vary with the degree of study risk, researchers need to specify these levels beforehand.

Dr. L is an investigator at a large university. He is seeking approval to recruit subjects for a new protocol that he has developed. The study targets subjects with severe depression, entails a moderate degree of risk, and has a high potential for direct therapeutic benefit. Assignment to groups will be random, and a crossover design will be used. Given the subject population, the moderate degree of risk, and the high potential for benefit, Dr. L reasons that subjects should be able to demonstrate understanding of at least 80% of the information they are told; be able to appreciate the risks, benefits, and consequences of participation; and engage in at least low-level reasoning. He instructs his assistants that all subjects must understand that 1) the protocol will involve 10 visits to the hospital, each lasting 1 hour; 2) blood will be drawn on each of these visits; 3) initial assignment to groups is random, but each group will be given the experimental medium at some point; and 4) the primary risk is agitation as a side effect of the medication.

Third, the consent process itself needs to be structured to allow assessment of subject capacity. The staff in charge of recruitment must be informed of the standards that have been decided on and instructed how to apply them. Moreover, a process of assessment, either formal or informal, should be specified. At present, an informal process (i.e., the research assistant judges the relevant capacities during individual interactions) is permissible because no validated tools for formal assessment exist. However, if effective screening tools are developed in the future, they may take the place of less formal approaches. Furthermore, research staff should be monitored for adherence to the competence assessment protocol. Because implementation of such a protocol may conflict with the aim of recruiting as many subjects as possible, targets can be employed to establish reasonable percentages of subjects who should be excused from the consent process because of incompetence. For example, for a given subject population, an investigator may be aware that a certain percentage of individuals (e.g., 10%) are likely to be incompetent. This percentage should be used to guide the research assistant who is recruiting subjects. That is, the rates of potential subjects from whom consent was not solicited (in this example, 10%) should reflect the probable incidence of incompetence in the subject population. Research assistants need to be encouraged to exclude such subjects from the sample.

Dr. L's study has been approved, and subject recruitment has begun. In reviewing the initial subjects recruited, Dr. L notices that one research assistant has a 100% inclusion rate, whereas the other has a 90% inclusion rate. Because they are both drawing from the same population, Dr. L reviews recruitment procedures with his assistants. He makes it clear that he expects that a certain number of potential subjects approached will not have the capacity to consent and should not be included. He asks both assistants to carefully review the subjects they have included thus far and make sure they meet all of the requirements. When recruitment is complete, approximately 9% of all potential subjects approached are excluded because of incapacity. This figure is what Dr. L initially expected, and he notes this information in his subsequent write-up.

Finally, investigators need to make efforts to compensate for impairments detected. When impaired subjects are identified, they should not be excluded automatically from a study. Decision-making abilities are not fixed but highly context dependent. Investigators can take a number of steps to both compensate for decision-making impairment and safeguard impaired subjects who are enrolled in a protocol.

Many studies now suggest that modifications of disclosure methods can significantly improve potential subjects' understanding (Benson et al. 1988; Cournos 1993; Grisso et al. 1995; Tymchuk et al. 1988). For example, the temporal dimension for obtaining consent may be important. Severely disordered patients may need repetitive disclosures (Munetz et al. 1982). Even subjects who are not cognitively impaired have a tendency to forget information and do not always understand when something is explained to them for the first time (Jaffe 1986). Using long consent forms or giving too much information at one time can be confusing (Grisso and Appelbaum 1995; Silva and Sorrell 1988). It is particularly important that the investigator ask questions at different points during the disclosure to assess the subject's understanding so that corrective steps can be taken if necessary. In addition, a number of aids to increase understanding can be employed, such as videotaped disclosures to augment discussion with researchers and employment of independent educators whose sole job is to teach subjects about the studies to which they are being asked to consent (Benson et al. 1988). Investigators may also attempt to convey pertinent information with the aid of other persons such as the subject's family. Subjects should be given information to take home, read, think about, and discuss with others and then have an opportunity to return to have their questions answered.

In addition to previously mentioned aids to understanding, more severely impaired subjects may need supplemental safeguards. It is important to acknowledge that some important research questions may never be answerable without involving subjects with severe and irremediable decision-making impairments. For example, studies aimed at discovering treatments for schizophrenia or Alzheimer's disease necessitate inclusion of subjects with those disorders, many of whom are impaired. We need creative approaches to authorizing surrogate decision makers to act for subjects in a manner protective of their interests (American College of Physicians 1989; Berg 1996; Keyserlingk et al. 1995). One example is the present National Institutes of Health (NIH) Clinical Center policy of using the durable power of attorney prospectively to authorize research with incompetent Alzheimer's patients (Fletcher et al. 1985). Another is the use of a Ulysses Contract, or self-binding psychiatric advance directive authorizing research participation (DeRenzo 1994a). A definitive resolution of this problem will be difficult because many of the issues involved are subject to state laws that vary widely (DeRenzo 1994b). Even so, various solutions are possible, and mechanisms can be adapted for implementation in different jurisdictions.

CONCLUSION

Subject capacity to consent to research has become a focal point for heated discussions among investigators, subject populations, and families. The judiciary, too, has been drawn into the fray, as evidenced by recent cases in New York and Texas (*T.D. v. New York State Office of Mental Health* 1997; Flynn 1995). Clearly, biomedical research is necessary if we are to find treatments and possibly cures for some of the most devastating illnesses that exist in our society (e.g., schizophrenia and AIDS). Investigators should be permitted to conduct such research, and individuals who are interested should be allowed, and perhaps even encouraged, to participate. Yet the populations involved in such research are among the most vulnerable in our society. Although we are interested in allowing these individuals the same freedom to make choices as other members of our society, we are concerned about protecting persons whose capacity to make decisions autonomously is impaired. The suggestions in this chapter will not resolve all of the difficult issues (e.g., should incompetent subjects be permitted to participate in high-risk/low-direct-benefit protocols?); they will, however, aid in our understanding of subject capacity in the context of biomedical research. Moreover, they should help us to identify impaired subjects and to develop mechanisms designed to deal with those impairments.

REFERENCES

American College of Physicians: Cognitively impaired subjects. Ann Intern Med 111:843-848, 1989

Appelbaum PS: Rethinking the conduct of psychiatric research. Arch Gen Psychiatry 54:117-120, 1997

Appelbaum PS, Grisso T: Assessing patients' capacities to consent to treatment. N Engl J Med 319:1635-1638, 1988

Appelbaum PS, Grisso T: The MacArthur Treatment Competence Study, I: mental illness and competence to consent to treatment. Law and Human Behavior 19:105-126, 1995

Appelbaum PS, Lidz CW, Meisel A: Informed Consent: Legal Theory and Clinical Practice. New York, Oxford University Press, 1987a

Appelbaum PS, Roth LH: Competency to consent to research: a psychiatric overview. Arch Gen Psychiatry 39:951-958, 1982

Appelbaum PS, Roth LH, Lidz CW: The therapeutic misconception: informed consent in psychiatric research. Int J Law Psychiatry 5:319-329, 1982

Appelbaum PS, Roth LH, Lidz CW, et al: False hopes and best data: consent to research and the therapeutic misconception. Hastings Cent Rep 17:20-24, 1987b

Benson PR, Roth LH, Appelbaum PS, et al: Information disclosure, subject understanding, and informed consent in psychiatric research. Law and Human Behavior 12:455-476, 1988

Berg JW: The legal and ethical complexities of consent with cognitively impaired research subjects: proposed guidelines. Journal of Law, Medicine, and Ethics 24:18-35, 1996

Berg JW, Appelbaum PS, Grisso T: Constructing competence: formulating standards of legal competence to make medical decisions. Rutgers Law Review 48:345-396, 1996

Bonnie RJ: The competence of criminal defendants: beyond Dusky and Drope. University of Miami Law Review 47:539-601, 1993

Bonnie RJ: Research with cognitively impaired subjects: unfinished business in the regulation of human research. Arch Gen Psychiatry 54:105-111, 1997

Candilis PJ, Wesley RW, Wichman A: A survey of researchers using a consent policy for cognitively impaired human research subjects. IRB: Review of Human Subjects Research 15(6):1-4, 1993

Carpenter WT, Bartko JJ, Carpenter CL, et al: Another view of schizophrenia subtypes: a report from the International Pilot Study of Schizophrenia. Arch Gen Psychiatry 33:508-516, 1976

Cassel C: Ethical issues in the conduct of research in long term care. Gerontologist 28:90-96, 1988

College on Problems of Drug Dependence: Human subject issues in drug abuse research. Drug Alcohol Depend 37:167-175, 1995

Cournos F: Do psychiatric patients need greater protection than medical patients when they consent to treatment? Psychiatr Q 64:319-329, 1993

Cummings J, Benson DF: Dementia: A Clinical Approach. Boston, MA, Butterworth-Heinemann, 1992

Department of Health and Human Services: Rules and Regulations for the Protection of Human Research Subjects, 45 Code of Federal Regulations §§46.101-46.409 (1991)

DeRenzo EG: The ethics of involving psychiatrically impaired persons in research. IRB: Review of Human Subjects Research 16(6): 7-9, 11, 1994a

DeRenzo E: Surrogate decision making for severely cognitively impaired research subjects: the continuing debate. Camb Q Healthcare Ethics 3:539-548, 1994b

Drane JF: Competency to give an informed consent: a model for making clinical assessments. JAMA 252:925-927, 1984

Elliott C: Caring about risks: are severely depressed patients competent to consent to research? Arch Gen Psychiatry 54:113-116, 1997

Evans DA, Funkenstein HH, Albert MS, et al: Prevalence of Alzheimer's disease in a community population of older persons. JAMA 262:2551-2556, 1989

Fitten LJ, Waite MS: Impact of medical hospitalization on treatment decision-making capacity in the elderly. Arch Intern Med 150:1717-1721, 1990

Fletcher JC, Dommel FW, Cowell DD: A trial policy for the intramural programs of the National Institutes of Health: consent to research with impaired human subjects. IRB: Review of Human Subjects Research 7(6):1-6, 1985

Flynn G: Suit challenges involuntary use of mental patients. Houston Chronicle, August 22, 1995, p A12

Grisso T, Appelbaum PS: The MacArthur Treatment Competence Study, III: abilities of patients to consent to psychiatric and medical treatment. Law and Human Behavior 19:149-174, 1995

Grisso T, Appelbaum PS, Mulvey E, et al: The MacArthur Treatment Competence Study, II: measures of abilities related to competence to consent to treatment. Law and Human Behavior 19:127-148, 1995

High D, Whitehouse PJ, Post SG, et al: Guidelines for addressing ethical and legal issues in Alzheimer disease research: a position paper. Alzheimer Dis Assoc Disord 8:66-74, 1994

Jaffe R: Problems of long-term informed consent. Bull Am Acad Psychiatry Law 14:163-169, 1986

Keyserlingk EW, Glass K, Kogan S, et al: Proposed guidelines for the participation of persons with dementia as research subjects. Perspect Biol Med 38:319-362, 1995

Kleber HD: Drug abuse liability testing: human subject issues, in Testing for Abuse Liability of Drugs in Humans (NIDA Research Monograph Series No 92). Edited by Fichman MW, Mello NK. Washington, DC, National Institute on Drug Abuse, 1989, pp 341-356

Marks ES, Derderian SS, Wray HL: Guidelines for conducting HIV research with human subjects at a U.S. military medical center. IRB: Review of Human Subjects Research 14(1):7-10, 1992

Marson DC, Schmitt FA, Ingram KK, et al: Determining the competency of Alzheimer patients to consent to treatment and research. Alzheimer Dis Assoc Disord 8(suppl 4):5-18, 1994

Morreim EH: Competence: at the intersection of law, medicine, and philosophy, in Competency: A study of Informal Competency Determinations in Primary Care. Edited by Cutter MAG, Shelp EE. Dordrecht, The Netherlands, Kluwer, 1991, pp 93-125

Munetz MR, Roth LH, Cornes CL: Tardive dyskinesia and informed consent: myths and realities. Bull Am Acad Psychiatry Law 10:77-88, 1982

National Commission for the Protection of Human Subjects of Biomedical and Behavioral Research: The Belmont Report: Ethical Principles and Guidelines for the Protection of Human Subjects of Research (DHEW Publ No OS-78-0012). Washington, DC, U.S. Government Printing Office, 1978

Overall JE, Gorham DR: The Brief Psychiatric Rating Scale. Psychol Rep 10:799-812, 1962

President's Commission for the Study of Ethical Problems in Medicine and Biomedical and Behavioral Research: Making Health Care Decisions: A Report on the Ethical and Legal Implications of Informed Consent in the Patient-Practitioner Relationship, Vol 1: Report. Washington, DC, Superintendent of Documents, October 1982

Regier DA, Narrow WE, Rae DS, et al: The de facto US mental and addictive disorders service system: epidemiologic catchment area prospective 1-year prevalence rates of disorders and services. Arch Gen Psychiatry 50:85-94, 1993

Riecken HW, Ravich R: Informed consent to biomedical research in Veterans Administration hospitals. JAMA 248:344-348, 1982

Rosenfeld B, Turkheimer E, Gardner W: Decision making in a schizophrenic population. Law and Human Behavior 16:651-662, 1992

Roth LH, Lidz CW, Meisel A, et al: Competency to decide about treatment or research: an overview of some empirical data. Int J Law Psychiatry 5:29-50, 1982

Roth LH, Meisel A, Lidz CW: Tests of competency to consent to treatment. Am J Psychiatry 134:279-280, 1977

Sachs GA, Stocking CB, Stern R, et al: Ethical aspects of dementia research: informed consent and proxy consent. Clinical Research 42:403-412, 1994

Salgo v Leland Stanford Junior University Board of Trustees, 317 P2d 170 (1957)

Schachter D, Kleinman I, Prendergast P, et al: The effect of psychopathology and the ability of schizophrenic patients to give informed consent. J Nerv Ment Dis 182:360-362, 1994

Schloendorff v Society of New York Hospital, 105 NE 92 (NY 1914)

Shamoo AE, Irving DN: Accountability in research using persons with mental illness. Accountability in Research 3:1-17, 1993

Silva MC, Sorrell JM: Enhancing comprehension of information for informed consent: a review of empirical research. IRB: Review of Human Subjects Research 10(1):1-5, 1988

Simes RJ, Tattersall MH, Coates AS, et al: Randomized comparison of procedures for obtaining informed consent in clinical trials of treatment for cancer. BMJ 293:1065-1068, 1986

Speer DC: Comorbid mental and substance disorders among the elderly: conceptual issues and propositions. Behavior, Health, and Aging 1:163-171, 1990

Stanley B, Guido J, Stanley M, et al: The elderly patient and informed consent. JAMA 252:1302-1306, 1984

Stanley B, Stanley M, Guido J, et al: The functional competency of elderly at risk. Gerontologist 28:53-58, 1988

Stanley B, Stanley M, Lautin A, et al: Preliminary findings on psychiatric patients as research participants: a population at risk? Am J Psychiatry 138:669-671, 1981

Stanley B, Stanley M, Peselow E, et al: The effects of psychotropic drugs on informed consent. Psychopharmacology 18:102-104, 1982

Stanley B, Stanley M, Stein J, et al: Psychopharmacologic treatment and informed consent: empirical research. Psychopharmacol Bull 21:110-113, 1985

T.D. v New York State Office of Mental Health, 690 N.E. 2d 1259 (N.Y. 1997)

Tymchuk AJ, Ouslander JG, Rahbar B, et al: Medical decision-making among elderly people in long-term care. Gerontologist 28(suppl):59-63, 1988

White PD, Denise SH: Medical treatment decisions and competency in the eyes of the law: a brief survey, in Competency: A Study of Informal Competency Determinations in Primary Care. Edited by Cutter MAG, Shelp EE. Dordrecht, The Netherlands, Kluwer, 1991, pp 149-166

Wilson WH, Ban TA, Guy W: Flexible system criteria in chronic schizophrenia. Compr Psychiatry 27:259-265, 1986